YOUTH BIBLE STUDY GUIDE

Sin, Forgiveness and Eternal Life

Youth Bible Study Guides

Sexuality

Following God

Image and Self-Esteem

Peer Pressure

Father God

Jesus Christ and the Holy Spirit

Sin, Forgiveness and Eternal Life

Church, Prayer and Worship

Sharing Your Faith

Tough Times

Money and Giving

Hunger, Poverty and Justice

YOUTH BIBLE STUDY GUIDE

Sin, Forgiveness and Eternal Life

COMPILED AND WRITTEN BY

CHIP AND HELEN KENDALL

Authentic

First published 2014 by Authentic Media Ltd
Presley Way, Crownhill, Milton Keynes, MK8 0ES.
www.authenticmedia.co.uk

British Library Cataloguing in Publication Data
A catalogue record for this book is available from the British Library

ISBN-13: 978-1-86024-634-0

Extracts taken from:
Andy Flannagan, *God 360°*, Spring Harvest and Authentic, 2006
Chip Kendall, *The Mind of chipK: Enter at Your Own Risk*, Authentic, 2005
Vince Woltjer and Tim Vandenberg, *To Be Honest With You*, Authentic, 2005
Amanda Lord and Simon Lord, *Search for a Father*, Authentic, 2006
Keith Tondeur, *Street Parables for Today*, Authentic, 2004
Jenny Baker, *Transforming Prayer*, Spring Harvest and Authentic, 2004
Ems Hancock and Ian Henderson, *Sorted?*, Spring Harvest and Authentic, 2006
Russell Rook and Aaron White, *The Hitchhiker's Guide to the Kingdom*,
Spring Harvest and Authentic, 2007

Cover and page design by Temple Design
Cover based on a design by Beth Ellis
Printed in Great Britain by Bell and Bain, Glasgow

He died for all so that those who live would not continue to live for themselves. He died for them and was raised from death so that they would live for him.

(2 Corinthians 5:15)

Chip and Helen Kendall are Creative Arts Pastors at Audacious Church, Manchester, and also love spending as much time as possible with their kids, Cole, Eden and Elliot. They currently reside in Stockport, England and they still have trouble understanding each other's accents.

Chip tours the world, fronting the Chip Kendall band. His album *Holy Freaks* and first book, *The Mind of chipK: Enter at Your Own Risk* has helped loads of young people grow in their faith. He's also the driving force behind a new youth media movement called MYvoice with Cross Rhythms, as well as being a regular presenter on GodTV. All of these jobs continue to pave the way for him to speak at events everywhere. www.chipkendall.com

After working for ten years as a dancer and tour/bookings manager, Helen now juggles looking after the kids with her work at Audacious Church helping to develop dance and all things creative. She also enjoys doing some writing and project management. Helen loves the variety in her life, and no two days are ever the same.

Guest writer, Ben Jack
Through his role as director of the resourcing organization Generation Now, and as a speaker and author, Ben is committed to helping youth and young adults question, evaluate, understand and live for a faith in Jesus. Ben is passionate about exploring narrative – particularly through film – and the role of story in our faith and lives, as well as culture, philosophy and theology. Ben is also known as award-winning DJ and producer Galactus Jack. www.ben-jack.com / www.generation-now.co.uk

Thank Yous
Massive thanks to Malcolm Down, Liz Williams and the rest of the gang at Authentic Media for giving us the opportunity to work on these study guides . . . it's been a blast. To everyone at SFC who read the books and gave us your thoughts, we appreciate the feedback. Thanks to everyone at Audacious Church for being an amazing church family. Thanks to lovely Lucy West for the fantastic photos and Lucy Wells for the typing. To everyone who talked to Chip for the 'people clips', thanks for your honesty and willingness to put up with the quirky questions. A really huge thank you to Brian and Norma Wilson for their 'hidden pearls' of wisdom. We loved your perspective on things. Finally, big thanks to all the authors whose work we have used in this book. You are an inspiration.

CONTENTS

INSTRUCTIONS

The book you're holding in your hands is a study guide. It's a compilation of extracts from lots of other books written about this subject. It might not make you the world's expert on the subject, but it should give you lots of useful information and, even better, it should give you some idea of what the Bible has to say about . . . SIN, FORGIVENESS AND ETERNAL LIFE.

What is a 'reaction box'?

Throughout the book, you'll find these helpful little reaction boxes. We've added them so that you can decide for yourself what you think about what you've just read. Here's what one should look like once you've filled it in:

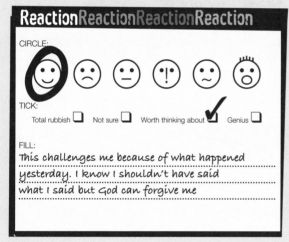

ReactionReactionReactionReaction

CIRCLE:

TICK:

Total rubbish ☐   Not sure ☐   Worth thinking about ✔   Genius ☐

FILL:

This challenges me because of what happened yesterday. I know I shouldn't have said what I said but God can forgive me

Pretty simple really . . .

Circle the face that reflects how you feel about it.

Tick the box that shows what you think about it.

Fill in any thoughts you have about what you've learned on the lines provided.

What are 'people clips'?

Just so you don't get too bored, we've added a bunch of 'people clips' to each study guide. These are people just like you, who were happy for us to pick their brains about various related topics. Who knows? Maybe you'll find someone you recognize.

What are 'hidden pearls'?

Everyone needs some good old-fashioned 'grandparently' advice, so we collected some pearls of wisdom from our friends Brian and Norma Wilson, which you can find scattered throughout the book.

What is a 'reality check'?

Finally, throughout the book you will come across sections called 'Reality check'. These should provide a chance for you to apply what you've been learning to your own life experiences.

Other than that, the only rule that applies when reading this book is that you HAVE FUN! So start reading.

Chip & Helen

Introduction

Imagine if you lived in a society where there were no rules and no consequences. You could lie in bed as long as you wanted, you could go to school or work only if you felt like it, you could take someone else's money to get yourself lunch. You could tell lies and no one could stop you, you could go shopping and help yourself to whatever you liked and then grab someone else's car and get yourself home. Of course this would all be great until people did the same to you! Maybe you wear your favourite top to school and someone takes it, or while you are on your new iPhone someone else helps themselves. Or you get home to find that your room is empty because someone else has nicked your furniture and there is nothing you can do about it. Now it might be just me, but although no rules and consequences sounds good to start with, when you think about it, not much time would have to go by before life would become pretty rubbish, with society breaking down completely. Think of what you would lose. There would be no justice, no peace, no security, no trust.

Some people think God is a giant tyrant up in the sky with a big stick, dishing out rules just for the sake of being mean and then bashing people over the head and sending them to hell when they don't keep to them. Other people think God is this nice, fuzzy old man in the sky who will overlook the odd white lie that they tell, or the occasional lustful thought or proud attitude and just let them into heaven because they are a 'good person'. **THE BIBLE PAINTS A DIFFERENT PICTURE OF GOD ALTOGETHER**. This book looks at sin, forgiveness and eternal life, which all tie together to help us figure out what God is really like. Sin is the stuff we do wrong when we break the good and just laws that God has set up. Forgiveness is God's way of dealing with our sin, and how we spend eternal life is the long-term consequence of sin and forgiveness. What we believe about these things forms the foundation of our faith as Christians, so it's definitely worth having a good look at what the Bible has to say about them.

Sin and Temptation

The sinful self wants what is against the Spirit,
and the Spirit wants what is against the sinful self.
They are always fighting against each other,
so that you don't do what you really want to do.

(Galatians 5:17)

First up

It's ugly, it's hairy, it's probably got one eye and six legs and you're pretty sure it's lurking somewhere just out of sight under your bed. You lie awake at night listening out for that tell-tale creak or groan that will make you run for cover under your favourite Buzz Lightyear duvet. You peep slowly out from your hiding place. Are those shadows moving on the wall? And that funny shape next to the wardrobe, is it just your dressing gown, or a monster?!

OK, so maybe you're too old to believe in monsters under the bed or in the back of the closet, but for many of us sin is just as ugly, hairy and scary and it can make us want to hide under the covers and hope it will go away. If you are like us, it's easy to think you are the only one in the world who struggles with your sinful self. When we look at other Christians somehow they always seem to have it all together, or at least more together than us. You know that you look OK on the outside, but if people really knew what you were like there would be trouble, right? If they really knew what went on in your head or behind closed doors, they would think differently. Maybe you battle with temptation and feel like you aren't strong enough to stand up to it and that no one else in the world keeps giving in like you do.

Let's get real. Everyone struggles with sin. Some sins are obvious and have big consequences, others are hidden thoughts and attitudes that are less easily detected. One thing you can be sure of is that you are not alone. No matter how bad you think you are there will definitely be lots of other people struggling with the same things you struggle with. Or maybe you reckon you are quite a good person actually: you've never murdered anyone, you don't steal or get drunk, you are doing quite nicely. The Bible makes it clear that we all sin. The Holy Spirit in us battles against our sinful desires; we are in a fight. Whether you feel you are the worst of sinners or quite a holy person, we hope this chapter will challenge you and encourage you. Maybe it will challenge your idea of sin and what it is. Hopefully it will encourage you to keep on fighting temptation and trying to live a holy life like Jesus. It's time to start dealing with the hairy monster under the bed.

Original SIN

Helen talks

Let's go back to the beginning and think about what sin is. When the Bible uses the word sin, it simply means the wrong things that we do. That means that sin can be absolutely anything we do, on purpose or by mistake, that goes against God's way of doing things. God is perfect, just and righteous and never does anything wrong. So, every time we do anything that doesn't match up to his perfect standard, we are sinning. A sin could be as big as murdering someone or as small as wishing that you had that nice new iPad that your friend just got for their birthday. It could be stealing a million pounds, telling a little lie or getting angry with your mum. As Christians we often rate different sins and think that some are worse than others. We think, 'I'm a good person, I've never killed anyone and I don't swear or steal things,' but in reality, being prideful, or selfish, or not helping the poor, or having bitter thoughts about someone, or gossiping are sins, just like murder or stealing. When we do wrong stuff it hurts God, it separates us from him. It doesn't matter what the sin is, whether it's an obvious one or something that is easier to hide. Of course some sins have bigger consequences in our lives than others. If I go shoplifting and get caught I will pay the consequences with a criminal record, fine or possible prison sentence. If I gossip about a friend, the initial consequences will not be as big. However, all sin ultimately has the same consequence – separation from God.

ou might be wondering where sin came from and if God is so perfect and clever why he doesn't just stop us from sinning? To answer this question we need to go right back to the beginning. When God made people (check out Genesis chapter 1 and 2) he created them with free will – the ability to choose to do what was good or what was bad. That meant that they could choose to love and obey God, or to turn their backs on him and do things their own way. **GOD WANTED A PEOPLE WHO CHOSE TO LOVE HIM**, rather than a race of robots who only loved him because he designed them to, he wanted relationship with people, so he took the risk of giving them free will and only one rule that they couldn't break. As you probably already know, it wasn't long before Adam and Eve, the first humans, made the wrong choice and chose to disobey God (check out Genesis 3). For the first time in the short history of humanity a barrier was made between God and Adam and Eve. Being completely holy, God could no longer associate himself in the same way with sinful Adam and Eve, so he sent them away. Ever since then all people have struggled with the sinful nature inside them.

Now before you get really depressed and start to wonder how you will ever stop yourself from sinning a million times a day, remember that because of Jesus we have forgiveness for all our sins. God wanted a relationship with us, so he sent Jesus to die for all our sins (more about that in the Life Lesson on Forgiveness). **NOW, NO MATTER HOW MANY TIMES WE MESS UP WE CAN ASK FOR GOD'S FORGIVENESS** and because Jesus took the punishment for our sins on the cross we can be forgiven. We can have a relationship with God once again, without sin blocking our way, just like it was always meant to be since the beginning.

ReactionReactionReactionReaction

CIRCLE:

TICK:

Total rubbish ☐   Not sure ☐   Worth thinking about ☐   Genius ☐

FILL:

....

....

Criminal Master Mind

Chip talks

Imagine this:

Y ou're watching TV late at night. It's a slightly violent programme with a couple of dodgy sex scenes thrown in as well. During one particular fight sequence, you recall your so-called friend who'd spread a rumour about you earlier that day. You think, 'Boy, I wish I could tear them apart like that.' Then when one of the juicy sex scenes begins to unfold, you think, 'I know I should probably turn this off right now, but this is really turning me on . . .'

Just then, the sound of your front door being smashed in makes you jump to your feet. Floodlights pour in from every window, and the roar of helicopters above your roof fills the air. Eight fully armed SWAT team agents suddenly burst into your living room, shouting for you to get down on the floor and put your hands behind your head. When you do, the commander bends down, puts his knee on your back, leans in close to your ear and says,

'YOU'VE JUST BEEN CAUGHT BY THE SIN POLICE!'

OK, I know what you're probably thinking. 'That's ridiculous. No way would that ever happen.' And you're probably right. As far as I know no one has invented a CCTV camera for people's thought life yet. But nevertheless, according to the Bible all criminal activity – big or small – begins in the heart. Sin is a heart problem and it needs a heart solution.

CRIMINAL MASTER QUIZ

How many of the 10 commandments (God's Law) can you list here? (Hint: the full list can be found in Exodus 20:3–17)

1. ....

2. ....

3. ....

4. ....

5. ....

6. ....

7. ....

8. ....

9. ....

10. ....

A lot of people think that Jesus came to somehow make God's Law less harsh, but according to Matthew 5:17–28 he took it one step further! What does he say?

....

According to your understanding so far of what the Bible has to say about sin, in your opinion when does a temptation become a sin?

....

ReactionReactionReactionReaction

CIRCLE:

TICK:

Total rubbish ☐   Not sure ☐   Worth thinking about ☐   Genius ☐

FILL:

....

....

Get yourself to a high place of some description. This could be the top of a hill or a building. A cliff would be perfect.

Read Luke 4:1–13

For anyone who is gifted in certain ways (and that's all of us), it is very easy to rely on those gifts and talents, and not on God. There is a sense of that in what Jesus is being tempted to do in this passage. All that he was asked to do, he could have done. This story provides the subtext for U2's great song 'Vertigo' from *How to Dismantle an Atomic Bomb*. The vertigo Bono is experiencing comes from being up in that high place and hearing the words 'All this can be yours . . .'

THE BOTTOM LINE IS THAT SATAN ISN'T STUPID. He doesn't try to tempt us with what he knows we won't do (usually because of social constraints). He may not tempt us to hit someone, but he will perhaps tempt us to gossip about them. He may not tempt us to order a dodgy satellite channel, but he may tempt us to leave our eyes hovering over an unhelpful music video. He works by subtle increments.

We have oversimplified and dramatized the events in the desert. Satan doesn't appear in a puff of smoke wearing red leather and holding a pitchfork. Instead **HE SIDLES UP TO JESUS AS A PIOUS COUNSELLING FRIEND**, quoting Scripture. It is only at the end of temptation three that he is unmasked, offering a bribe, which he doesn't even attempt to wrap up with a spiritual contortion. All our temptation scenarios will probably start with a person or a situation that seems totally rational and respectable, rather than a bloke with horns, or large red Xs appearing in the corner of our vision to warn of impending danger.

PUT YOURSELF IN SATAN'S SHOES AND DRAW UP A MASTER PLAN on his behalf for how best to tempt you towards or away from certain things. Being an expert on the subject, you probably won't get it far wrong. This will bring some honesty and reality to your 'tempted' life. The best generals or sports coaches study their opponents' strategy at length. Share this plan with an accountable friend, who can help you watch out for the high tackles. This is something we need to talk about a lot, rather than pretend that we are immune from temptation, which is total nonsense, bearing in mind that even Jesus was tempted.

Jesus presented a dead straight bat to Satan's temptations by quoting Scripture. Would you be able to quote any verses of Scripture in the direction of the bowler? As a cricketer, it takes hard work and practice to develop the unnatural habit of playing straight, and it takes genuine effort to memorize some Scripture. (As with cricket, it's much easier just to have a swing.) Write out three verses on bits of paper that you will try and memorize during the course of today.

Andy Flannagan, *God 360°*, Spring Harvest Publishing and Authentic Media, 2006

ReactionReactionReactionReaction

CIRCLE:

TICK:

Total rubbish ☐   Not sure ☐   Worth thinking about ☐   Genius ☐

FILL:

....

....

....

....

Question Time

Chip talks

Why do I sin?
Good question. According to the Bible, sin is natural. **EVERYONE SINS. IT'S PART OF WHAT MAKES US HUMAN BEINGS**. In the history of the world, only one person has ever gone their whole lives without sinning. That's because he was 100% human and 100% God. I know, it sounds impossible. It's a tricky one to get your head around.

So if sin is only natural, why is it bad?
Sin is more than just natural. There are lots of natural things that are bad. Take cancer, for instance. It grows inside your body, unseen to the naked eye, and it can eventually kill you. Sin is a lot like cancer in that way. The Bible says that all sin leads to some kind of death. The difference between sin and cancer has to do with choice. Getting cancer isn't a choice. Sin is.

Is it ever right to sin?
No. Sin is sin. Full stop. **IT IS ALWAYS WRONG**. Trust me, I've lived longer than you have.

Then why would anyone ever choose to sin?
If only it was that easy! Ever since the very first human beings walked the earth, we've been choosing to sin. We like to break the rules. Even the Bible says that there is pleasure in sin . . . for a little while anyway. A little kid sneaks a hand into the cookie jar because he genuinely wants the cookie, not necessarily just because his mum tells him not to. There's always some sort of desire involved in sin.

So why do I want to sin?

Again, great question. In fact, you're not the first to ask that question. I still ask that question a lot. Temptation is something that isn't always easy to deal with. A couple of thousand years ago a guy named Paul wrote this:

I want to do what is good, but I don't do it. I don't do the good that I want to do. I do the evil that I don't want to do.

(Romans 7:18b–19)

Sounds confusing and pretty miserable to me. Like a fight you keep losing. But there is an answer.

What is the answer?

Well, you really need to read Romans chapter 7. The whole thing. It's kind of complicated, but first he concludes that it's actually the sin in him that wants to sin. Then he talks about being a prisoner in sin's war against him. And finally he recognizes that he needs someone to save him, and that person is Jesus. But you really need to read it for yourself.

ReactionReactionReactionReaction

CIRCLE:

☺ ☹ 😐 😲 😕 😮

TICK:

Total rubbish ☐   Not sure ☐   Worth thinking about ☐   Genius ☐

FILL:

....
....
....
....

Here is another extract looking at the temptation Jesus went through as he spent 40 days in the wilderness before starting his ministry. He was tempted directly by Satan, the Devil. Many of us won't experience temptation in such a direct way but it's useful to realize that Jesus has been through every temptation; he understands what it's like. You will never avoid all temptations, it's what you do with temptation that is important. The writer of this extract explains that sometimes we can feel like we can't beat certain sins and temptations in our lives, which is true, sometimes we can struggle for years with the same problems. However, God has still freed us from being slaves to sin and we belong to him. So here's an extract for all you thinkers out there. Check it out.

TEMPTATION

Read Luke 4:1–13

For centuries, theologians and laymen alike have struggled with giving meaningful credentials to the satanic grand inquisitor. Both scholars and ordinary folk have expressed cynicism about whether Satan's offer could have enticed the Son of God. As Jesus prepares for events that will later cause bloody sweat to drip off his forehead onto the soil of Gethsemane, the serpent promises Jesus nourishment of his physical needs, dominion over all kingdoms, and respite from the terrible sinful burden he would later carry on the cross. Although never questioning Satan's power to fulfil his proposal, Jesus clings to God's will and refuses to yield to the benefits of satanic authority.

Temptation plagues my chronically weakened spiritual immune system. Notwithstanding my best effort to fight the good fight, both my personal sin and our communal sin testify to Satan's power. While I camouflage many of my failings from public view, my hidden disease is far deadlier than any open wound. **SATAN AFFLICTS ME WITH EVERY ATTRACTIVE LIE**, referring often to a catalogue of my preferred temptations. I fall prey to those sins even though they ruin my prayer life. I leave the door open for the satanic ambassadors that depress me and detach me from God. Unlike David, I foolishly toss away my spiritual armour because it does not comfortably accommodate my evil companion. A pawn in spiritual warfare, **I CANNOT IMAGINE THE CRUSHING WEIGHT THAT SATAN BROUGHT DOWN UPON A TIRED AND HUNGRY JESUS.** Our Lord knows firsthand the depth of Satan's tempting power, that very influence that so quickly and completely overruns me.

More difficult to understand, I refuse to repudiate my friendship with sin. I pray earnestly, sometimes desperately, for God to remove my favourite sins from my life. However, even with the aid of prayer, I have not scrubbed my life clean with Jesus' blood. Nor terminated his dominion. I know that others, even people I admire as pillars of God's kingdom, struggle with a similar attachment to sin. While I have often heard speculation that the thorn Paul refers to was a physical handicap, I wonder if Paul's thorn was actually a deeply entrenched sin, a part of his former nature that he could not shake. I know neither the character of Paul's thorn nor why God does not remove my own, but I do understand that God has by his magnificent power freed me from slavery to Satan. Since God will use me for good despite my evil, I must persevere in faith, in hope, in prayer, and in a continuing expectation of freedom.

Vince Woltjer and Tim Vandenberg, *To Be Honest With You*, Authentic Media, 2005

ReactionReactionReactionReaction

CIRCLE:

TICK:

Total rubbish ☐   Not sure ☐   Worth thinking about ☐   Genius ☐

FILL:

....

....

....

....

Dealing with Sin and Temptation

Don't change yourselves to be like the people of this world, but let God change you inside with a new way of thinking. Then you will be able to understand and accept what God wants for you. You will be able to know what is good and pleasing to him and what is perfect.

(Romans 12:2)

First up

Imagine this: Johnny wakes up as his alarm sounds at 7.15 a.m. for school. He smiles to himself thinking of the day ahead, sits up in bed and sniffs his armpits to see if he needs a shower. They smell like roses so he bounces out of bed, irons his shirt, perfectly, gets dressed and skips down the stairs. After taking time to eat a nutritious breakfast he kisses his mum goodbye and leaves to get the bus for school. On his bus seat he finds a £5 note down a crack in the seat, which he responsibly hands in to the driver. He stops at the corner shop and waits outside to make sure he abides by the 'only 2 under 16s in the shop at any time' rule and then buys some sweets. Once in his classroom he meets up with his friends, none of whom have done their homework. They've come up with a cunning plan to avoid trouble: they are going to try to convince the sometimes-forgetful teacher that she didn't give them any homework. They just need Johnny to join in. But he doesn't. He tells them that lying is wrong, and when the teacher asks him, he tells the truth. At break time one of Johnny's friends offers to burn him a copy of a new album he just bought, but as Johnny knows that would be stealing, he declines the offer. At lunch time Johnny eats a balanced, healthy meal and avoids the extra helping of pudding. He works hard all afternoon, goes home to help his mum cook dinner and then sits down with his family for some educational conversation over dinner. He ends his day by doing his homework (all of it) and then laying out his clothes for the morning.

So what do you think of Johnny? Is he anything like you? How long do you think he could keep this up? Another day? A whole week? However much we would like God to make us into perfect people who say no to every temptation and float through life on a perfect cloud, it's not going to happen. In reality it can be much easier to sleep in, shout at our little sister, miss the bus, barge into the shop, walk on the grass, tell a little white lie about the homework, download illegal copies of music and so on. As Christians we are going to be constantly tempted to sin. The challenge is to learn to deal with it. We will never reach perfection, but that doesn't mean we should just give up and live however we feel. Read the Bible verse at the beginning of this Life Lesson again. It says, 'Don't change yourselves to be like the people of this world, but let God change you inside with a new way of thinking' (Romans 12:2). That takes some effort on our part. It's hard to not be shaped by this world's way of doing things and to change our thinking. We hope the extracts in this lesson will tell you more about how to move forward in the battle against sin.

Read Colossians 3:5–8

It's very easy to read these verses and think that they don't apply to us. These verses are only for the murderers and revellers of the world, surely? On closer examination, perhaps we are more a part of the story than we might imagine. Paul is writing to the Colossian church, after all. **THESE ARE WORDS INTENDED FOR PEOPLE JUST LIKE YOU AND ME**, and please don't try and tell me that we have somehow risen to a higher moral plane in the nineteen centuries since this letter was written.

Write each of the sins listed in the passage in the centre of a piece of A4 paper (one per page). Around the word, scribble the situations where you struggle with that particular sin. Spend a decent amount of time reflecting on each one, asking God to illuminate things that have settled to the back of your mind. Ask for and receive his forgiveness.

Paul exhorts the Colossians not to file away these sins, or micro-manage them, but to 'put them to death', so **DRAMATIC ACTION IS REQUIRED**. Gather up your sheets of paper and rip them up into tiny pieces. As you do, pray that the hold these things have on your life will disappear for good. If there are things that have come to light during this time, make sure you share them with someone else, so that they can help you with this part of your journey.

Andy Flannagan, *God 360°*, Spring Harvest Publishing and Authentic Media, 2006

ReactionReactionReactionReaction

CIRCLE:

😊 🙁 😐 😬 😏 😲

TICK:

Total rubbish ☐   Not sure ☐   Worth thinking about ☐   Genius ☐

FILL:

....

....

Lost and Found

chipK's mind

One of my favourite scenes in the *Lord of the Rings* trilogy takes place in the final movie *Return of the King*.

Location: *Top of Mount Doom*
Characters: *Frodo, Sam and Gollum*
Purpose: *To destroy the ring*

After having journeyed so far with Frodo, protecting him, and even carrying him along the way, Sam must watch in horror as Frodo and Gollum fight for possession of the ring. It was such a battle just to get this far, and now that it finally came right down to it, **FRODO COULDN'T LET GO OF THE VERY THING THAT WAS DESTROYING HIM**. Gollum proves to be the greedier of the two, as he bites the ring (and finger!) off Frodo's hand, falls into the hot molten lava, and finally dies with an evil grin on his face. Without the lure of the ring to distract him, Frodo finally comes to his senses and narrowly escapes with Sam to a new world and a new life.

AS A CHRISTIAN, I'M MEANT TO LOSE MY LIFE IN ORDER TO FIND IT.
That means letting go of my way of doing things in exchange for a relationship with Jesus. But, like Frodo and his ring, sometimes it's not so easy to throw down the things that mean so much to me. As Gollum would say, they're just too *precious* to me. And even though he loves me more than I know, even Jesus (like Sam) cannot make the decision for me. I must be determined to chuck my ring into the fire, and by doing so I can start a new life with the one who's been protecting and carrying me all along.

God's mind

'Those who love the life they have now will lose it. But whoever is willing to give up their life in this world will keep it. They will have eternal life.'
(John 12:25)

I have wandered away like a lost sheep. Come and find me. I am your servant, and I have not forgotten your commands.
(Psalm 119:176)

'Suppose one of you has 100 sheep, but one of them gets lost. What will you do? You will leave the other 99 sheep there in the field and go out and look for the lost sheep. You will continue to search for it until you find it. And when you find it, you will be very happy. You will carry it home, go to your friends and neighbours and say to them, "Be happy with me because I found my lost sheep!" In the same way, I tell you, heaven is a happy place when one sinner decides to change. There is more joy for that one sinner than for 99 good people who don't need to change.'

(Luke 15:4–7)

Your mind

- **How would I describe my relationship with Jesus at the moment?**

....
....

- **What is the 'ring' I often hold onto (my way of doing things)? Be specific:**

....
....

- **Three practical ways to 'lose' my life in this world:**
  1 ....
  2 ....
  3 ....

Chip Kendall, *The Mind of chipK: Enter at Your Own Risk*, **Authentic Media, 2006**

ReactionReactionReactionReaction

CIRCLE:

😊 🙁 😐 😯 😌 😲

TICK:

Total rubbish ☐   Not sure ☐   Worth thinking about ☐   Genius ☐

FILL:

....
....

Watch Out for LIONS!

Helen talks

Imagine this:

You spend ages on a big school project, really putting your best work into it. You get started on it early, do the research, include photos, quotes, the lot. Finally, after weeks of careful study you spell-check it, make sure it's all neat and tidy, print it out and put it in the teacher's tray feeling just a little bit proud of all your hard work. You're expecting a good grade, so you are surprised the next day when the teacher calls you over looking angry.

'What exactly do you mean by handing THIS in?' says the teacher, thrusting what looks like your project into your hand.

You're confused, you look at it and it's *like* your work, but different. Someone has obviously hacked into your computer and filled your work with spelling mistakes, deleted whole sections, put in the wrong pictures, and re-printed it. It's a mess! They've been really crafty and made it look like your work but worse. You're gutted.

The Bible tells a story in Matthew 13:24–29 like this, about a farmer who planted some seeds in a field and went home to wait for them to grow so he could harvest his crop. One night while he was asleep his enemy crept into the field and planted a load of weeds without him knowing. Very crafty!

In a chapter about sin, we must talk about the devil and his tactics. You need to remember that **IN THE BATTLE AGAINST SIN IT'S NOT JUST YOU AGAINST SIN – THERE IS ALSO AN ENEMY WHO IS OUT TO TRIP YOU UP.** It's his intention to steal, kill, destroy and ultimately separate you from God. We all know that sin and guilt are ideal ways to keep us from God. The devil is crafty, and this story reminds us that he may not always take the obvious approach. The enemy in the story didn't just come out and trample on the farmer's crops – he was much more subtle than that. The Bible offers this advice, 'Control yourselves and be careful! The devil is your enemy, and he goes around like a roaring lion looking for someone to attack and eat. Refuse to follow the devil. Stand strong in your faith. You know that your brothers and sisters all over the world are having the same sufferings that you have' (1 Peter 5:8–9).

- *Think about how you would react if you spotted a real live lion prowling around your house, growling.*

- *How can you relate this to how you can avoid sin and temptation?*

- *There is hope! Check out these verses from the Bible and write down how they make you feel.*

So give yourselves to God. Stand against the devil, and he will run away from you.

(James 4:7)

....

....

So, brothers and sisters, be careful that none of you has the evil thoughts that cause so much doubt that you stop following the living God. But encourage each other every day, while you still have something called 'today'. Help each other so that none of you will be fooled by sin and become too hard to change. We have the honour of sharing in all that Christ has if we continue until the end to have the sure faith we had in the beginning.

(Hebrews 3:12–14)

....

....

Our fight is not against people on earth. We are fighting against the rulers and authorities and the powers of this world's darkness. We are fighting against the spiritual powers of evil in the heavenly places. That is why you need to put on God's full armour. Then on the day of evil, you will be able to stand strong. And when you have finished the whole fight, you will still be standing.

(Ephesians 6:12–13)

....

....

Tempted

Ben talks

There was just too much choice! As a child, when it came to sweets, I was a notoriously slow chooser. My mum would sometimes leave me by the penny sweets to choose what I wanted while she browsed the magazines in the newsagent's – although she probably could have read the entire Bible in the time it took me to pick out what I wanted.

O n this particular day, I finally made my selection and wandered over to her, arm outstretched, with the bag of carefully counted-out penny sweets inside. As my mum turned to take the bag from me and pay for the sweets, she asked me a question. I don't remember what it was exactly, only that my response was unintelligible, as it is difficult to answer a question, with a mouth full of candy.

'Are you eating sweets?' My mum roared with horror.

I might have got away with it if I'd been clever enough to swallow before answering sheepishly, and with cheeks puffed out like a hamster storing food for later, *'Noo . . .'*

Now it wasn't exactly the crime of the century, but I was so embarrassed to have been caught doing something that I knew I shouldn't have – eating sweets without paying for them. The worst part was seeing my mum's reaction. I could tell how disappointed she was with my behaviour. Both she and I knew that I knew better than to do what I did. However, faced with such a wide choice of sweets and a limited budget, I succumbed to the temptation to squeeze a few extra into my mouth for my own satisfaction.

Temptation takes so many shapes and forms, and **WE ARE OFTEN FACED WITH A CHOICE OF DOING WHAT IS RIGHT BY GOD'S STANDARDS OR WHAT IS, PERHAPS, EASIER AND MORE DESIRABLE BY OUR OWN**. A quick scan of the daily news shows us that the negative consequences of submitting to temptation are often far more devastating than embarrassing your mum at the sweet shop.

Jesus lived a perfect life, and yet faced incredible temptation directly from Satan. Is it possible that we could live this way too? God hasn't just told us how to live, he empowers us with his Spirit to live this way, choosing holiness instead of selfishness. How might this kind of attitude towards temptation change our lives and impact the world?

Read Matthew 4:1–11. See also Genesis 3:1–13, Matthew 26:41, 1 Corinthians 10:13.

Reflect

• *What are the effects of succumbing to temptation*
  a) on your life?
  b) in the world?

• *God forgives us when we mess up, but he wants us to make good choices and to become holy. In what ways does he help us to do this, and how can we help each other?*

Respond

• *Think of a significant area of temptation in your life – something that comes up again and again. Share it with a trusted friend and pray about it, together and on your own, as often as possible. Ask your friend to lovingly hold you accountable for your actions in this area.*

Remember

• *We all face temptation, but confidence and trust in God will help you through.*

ReactionReactionReactionReaction

CIRCLE:

☺ ☹ 😐 😮 😌 😲

TICK:

Total rubbish ☐   Not sure ☐   Worth thinking about ☐   Genius ☐

FILL:

....

....

The Fireguard

Picture a fire on a cold winter's day

Feel the warmth that it gives

As the ice melts away.

See the leap of its flames

With the temperature rising

As it dances its call to you

Light, mesmerizing.

Drawing you close to its warming surround

Such tempting a welcome not easily found.

You would think it was safe

It would never do harm

But its glow, a façade, for such a deadly charm.

The life that it offers bears so great a cost

The more that you share with it, the more you have lost.

For it burns us with lies that it's safe – there's no fear

And consumes all that foolishly stray closer than near.

Like an army of locusts devour all in their way

Or a lion on the prowl its victim to slay.

There's no end to its fury, the burning within

Like a heart full of hatred, a life lost in sin.

So guard yourself from its touch, don't fuel the fire

Don't fall to temptation, resist the desire.

When the fuel of temptation is found in your way

The fire of sin, that leads us astray,

There's a face you can turn to

A fortress, a helper.

A guard from the flames, a healer, a shelter.

In his guard you are safe

From the flames that surround,

No scars from the burns

But life and new ground.

Amanda Lord and Simon Lord, *Search for a Father*, Authentic Media, 2006

ReactionReactionReactionReaction

CIRCLE:

TICK:

Total rubbish ☐   Not sure ☐   Worth thinking about ☐   Genius ☐

FILL:

....

....

....

....

I Thought CHRISTIANS DIDN'T DO That Sort of Thing!

Helen talks

Have you ever noticed that once you tell people that you are a Christian they expect you to be perfect? 'Oooh, you swore, I thought Christians didn't swear!' 'Weren't you drinking at that party last night? I thought Christians didn't get drunk!' Sometimes it can feel like your non-Christian friends are on a mission to point out what a bad Christian you are. The point is this – Christians aren't perfect! You don't become a Christian and then suddenly never sin again. A Christian is just someone who knows that they mess up all the time, but that if they ask Jesus to forgive them, they will be completely made right with God. But another really big point is that as a Christian you are representing Jesus and Christianity. Many of your friends will judge Jesus and Christianity based only on how you act. Quite a responsibility!

Let's be realistic, there are going to be times when, no matter how hard you try, you will do something that doesn't exactly represent Jesus in a good way. What do you do then? Give up on being a Christian because it's just too hard or because you are embarrassed that you went wrong and everyone knows about it? NO! Take it on the chin.

First, go to God and be honest, say, **'GOD, I'M SORRY, I DID THE WRONG THING, I'VE HURT YOU AND I'VE MADE YOU LOOK BAD IN FRONT OF PEOPLE.'**

But if we confess our sins, God will forgive us. We can trust God to do this. He always does what is right. He will make us clean from all the wrong things we have done.

(1 John 1:9)

Also check out Psalm 32:3–5.

Second, you need to go to your friends and be honest with them. Tell them that you did the wrong thing. Tell them you regret going against what you believe and that you are still a Christian and have been forgiven by God. It might be really difficult to admit that you went wrong but people will respect you for it.

Then of course comes the really difficult part – change your behaviour! If you go out to a party and get drunk, say sorry to God and your friends the next day and then go out and do the same thing every Friday for a month, no one will believe your apology. **YOU NEED TO LIVE UP TO THE STANDARDS GOD HAS SET.** Get some accountability, think practically about how you will avoid sinning again. If that sounds too hard then here's the good news: you don't have to do it alone. It would be impossible if we just had to achieve everything with our own willpower but instead God gives us the Holy Spirit to help us.

So I tell you, live the way the Spirit leads you. Then you will not do the evil things your sinful self wants.
(Galatians 5:16)

Ask the Holy Spirit to help you overcome sin. He can help you in every area of your life: thoughts, words, actions. Let the Holy Spirit lead you and help you to represent Christ the best way possible.

ReactionReactionReactionReaction

CIRCLE:

TICK:
Total rubbish ☐   Not sure ☐   Worth thinking about ☐   Genius ☐

FILL:

....
....
....
....

Reality Check

SIN STRUGGLES

Everyone struggles with different temptations. Write 10 things you struggle with in the box below – be honest. For example, pride, lust, stealing, jealousy, gossip, etc.

1. ....
2. ....
3. ....
4. ....
5. ....
6. ....
7. ....
8. ....
9. ....
10. ....

Are there places where you are more likely to fall into temptation to do these things, or are there people who encourage you to do them?
Fill them in below.

1. ....
2. ....
3. ....
4. ....
5. ....
6. ....
7. ....
8. ....
9. ....
10. ....

Write down the opposite to each of your temptations in the boxes below (e.g. instead of pride – humility; instead of gossip – trustworthiness; instead of stealing – giving).

1. ....
2. ....
3. ....
4. ....
5. ....

6. ....
7. ....
8. ....
9. ....
10. ....

Think of ways you can avoid putting yourself in situations where you usually give in to temptation and instead you can do the opposite. For example, if hanging round with particular people makes you feel important and proud in a bad way, try to become humble by hanging out with someone unpopular in school. Or, if a certain friend encourages you to gossip, try and battle that by spending time saying good things about other people instead. Fill in your ideas below.

1. ....
   ....
2. ....
   ....
3. ....
   ....
4. ....
   ....
5. ....
   ....

6. ....
   ....
7. ....
   ....
8. ....
   ....
9. ....
   ....
10. ....
    ....

It is impossible to beat sin on your own. Finish by asking God to forgive you for the sins you have listed. Then ask the Holy Spirit to help you say no to temptation and take the opposite path instead.

Names: Joel and Simon Consiglio

Ages: 22 and 21

Town: St Helen's

Passionate about: Music and God

What are your favourite sweets?

Joel: **Starburst**

Simon: **Mentos**

What do you think is wrong with children's television at the moment?

Simon: **They've got rid of some of the great shows like SuperTed. Bring SuperTed back! And Bananaman and Bodger & Badger!**

What toothpaste do you use?

Both: **Colgate**

How would you define 'sin'?

Joel: **Doing things your way rather than God's way.**

What is the best way to deal with sin?

Joel: **Make yourself accountable to someone who's a leader, and pray to God about it. Know how to deal with temptation.**

Simon: **Also, admit to God that you are wrong and choose to repent. It's important to be led by the Holy Spirit to repent.**

Who do you think is a good example of someone who says 'no' to the right things?

Both: **Our dad.**

Forgiveness

My dear friends, you always obeyed what you were taught. Just as you obeyed when I was with you, it is even more important for you to obey now that I am not there. So you must continue to live in a way that gives meaning to your salvation. Do this with fear and respect for God.

(Philippians 2:12)

√3

First up

So far in this book we have looked a lot at the bad stuff, at sin, at how impossible it is for us to match up to God's standard. Most world religions leave it at that. They leave it that we are responsible for making up for our sin, either by trying to live a perfect life, by paying some kind of penance, saying special prayers, going on pilgrimages or witnessing to a particular number of people. In all other religions people must work their way to God. Christianity is different. The difference is grace and forgiveness. As Christians we think it is madness to believe that we can be good enough for God, it's impossible, one mistake and we would be done for. The Bible says that because Jesus, a perfect man, died, he was able to take the punishment we deserved so we can walk free. He paid the fine, did the prison sentence, took our place so that we can have access to God's forgiveness. God now sees us through Jesus, he chooses to see the finished product. It means that every time we mess up we can be forgiven by God for whatever we have done if we say we are sorry and ask Jesus to be in charge of our lives.

Forgiveness is not just something that happens once, on the day of our salvation. The Bible says, 'Keep on working to complete your salvation with fear and trembling' (Philippians 2:12). We should come to God regularly and say sorry – repent – of the wrong things we have done. We should thank God for his forgiveness and then rejoice that he has thrown our sin far away.

What is the furthest possible place you could throw something before it started coming back?

Check out Psalm 103:12 and complete the verse below:

'He has taken our sins as far away from us...

....,'

In this Life Lesson we will look at some different aspects of forgiveness. First we will look at what God did by ultimately forgiving us when Jesus died on the cross. Then we will look at what we need to do – repentance or saying sorry to God and also at how we must follow God's example and forgive others.

Turn Around

Walk around a park (or any large area) via a circular route (lakes are good for this). Take in everything there is to see. Even if you are limited to circling your house, still do it.

Then turn around. Walk in the opposite direction. You may be amazed at how different the same place can look. You may notice buildings that weren't so obvious, the different emphases of colour, the changed backdrop of the sky, and the change in shadows.

Now read Acts 3:17–20. Your experience underlines the 'turning around' that is repentance. It is more than simply saying sorry. **IT IS A NEW WAY OF SEEING THE SAME LIFE.** In which of your life situations do you need to not just say sorry to God, but walk through them in a completely different direction?

If you struggle to truly 'turn around' in various situations, then join the club. Often our spiritual instincts aren't dissimilar to our physical instincts, and I see my reticence to 'turning around' most when I'm trying to navigate towards a destination. After missing a turning, I will stubbornly keep trying to find another way that is 'just as quick' rather than swallow my pride and head back in the opposite direction. It's about being honest and admitting mistakes, rather than trying to 'fix' things ourselves.

Ask God to show you what your 'new direction' will look like in various situations. It may mean not going near the TV late at night. It may mean not going near high street clothes stores. Whichever direction it is, enjoy the new view.

Andy Flannagan, *God 360°*, Spring Harvest Publishing and Authentic Media, 2006

ReactionReactionReactionReaction

CIRCLE:

😊 🙁 😐 ！ 😕 😮

TICK:

Total rubbish ☐ Not sure ☐ Worth thinking about ☐ Genius ☐

FILL:

....
....
....
....

Welcome Back

Read Luke 15:11–32

T here was a man who had two daughters. The elder, Kate, was content to work through school and go on to university but the younger one, Sally, was restless. 'I'm fed up with living here,' she used to shout at her parents. 'It's so boring. There's nothing to do and my friends never want to go anywhere. As for you, all you do is nag me to death: "Don't go there, don't mix with those people, and don't be late home." You don't love me. You just want to control me.'

Sally, who was fourteen, had seen kids her age having a great time on the television. SHE WANTED MONEY, THINGS AND FUN AND SHE WANTED THEM NOW. Her father had a jeweller's shop in the town where they lived and Sally used to work there on Saturdays. One day she offered to close the shop and bank the takings. Her father worried that she might be up to something as she was so impulsive and wanted things immediately. Obviously she would get a useful inheritance when he died, but if she wanted to take it now he would not stand in her way. So he left the shop early. But rather than do as she had promised, Sally took the cash and all the jewellery and fled north, where she sold it for thousands of pounds.

The money that she had with her enabled her to buy an extensive range of designer label clothes. She changed her hairstyle and had some body piercing and tattoos done. When she looked at herself in the mirror she did not recognize the little girl she had left behind. She was a young woman now, she proudly thought to herself. I don't need my dad to tell me what to do. Sally made friends by showering them with free clothes and drinks and it wasn't long before a man in his twenties took a keen interest in her. Soon they were living together in a flat that she was paying for. Within days he had taken over her life and started to control her money.

Sally lived like this every day, or more appropriately every night, throughout the summer. Her lover introduced her to drugs, soft ones to begin with, but she was soon hooked on crack. Not surprisingly, the lack of sleep and increasing drug use were both tiring and very expensive. By the end of the summer Sally realized that she was rapidly running out of money and she noticed that as this was happening all her so-called friends were disappearing just as fast. Soon only the man she loved was left. One day he announced in a matter of fact way that the money had run out and so she would have to start sleeping with men for money.

SALLY SPENT HER FIFTEENTH BIRTHDAY SATISFYING THE PERVERTED NEEDS OF A STRING OF MEN. Older and sicker now because of the drugs and degradation she was subjected to, she thought life could not get any worse than this. It was then that the man she believed loved her walked through the door with a new, 'fresher' model and she was simply thrown out onto the street. All she had were the clothes that she was just about wearing. Weeping, she huddled in a shop doorway, pulling some newspaper over herself to try and keep warm. As she did so, the name of her home town sprang out at her from the paper. Suddenly Sally came to her senses. 'I know I have blown it totally with my father,' she thought, 'but if I go back home at least I can be taken into care and get some medical attention. At the very least I must let my dad know I am alive.'

Twice when she rang home she got the answering machine. The third time she left a message. 'Dad, Mum. It's me. It's Sally. I'm so sorry for all the trouble I must have caused. I know I've blown it, but at least in my home town I can be taken into care and hopefully resurrect my school career. I'm going to be on a train that arrives tomorrow. Sorry once more. I will write to you when I'm there and explain to you all the terrible things I've done and what has happened to me.'

Sally had to do one last trick to get the train fare home. Soon she was recognizing the outskirts of her home town and she realized what she had thrown away. The train was pulling into the station now. It stopped and Sally stepped out.

Down the platform she could see her friends and then her mum and dad. Sally knew she had changed her appearance so much that no one would ever recognize her, but in the split second it took for her dad to see her he set off running down the platform as fast as he could go and swept her into his arms. Sally was crying but through her tears she saw that her dad was crying too. **SHE TRIED TO SAY 'SORRY' BUT WAS SMOTHERED IN KISSES**.

Again Sally tried to apologize. 'I don't deserve to have you here. I've done terrible things. I rebelled against you even though you loved me so much. I wanted money and nice things and I wanted it all immediately. I even wished you dead so I could get my hands on them.' But her father turned and called to her friends. 'Quick, come. Bring the new clothes we bought her. Take her to the hairdressers and let her smarten herself up. Spare no expense.' Then, turning to his daughter, he said, 'Every day since you left I've been searching for you, doing everything I could to find you. I'm so glad you've come back. Look, I have a ring to give you that was my mother's. Before she died she told me to give one to Kate and one to you when you had grown up. I think that day has arrived for you today. Now hurry. You don't want to be late for the party!'

Keith Tondeur, *Street Parables for Today*, Authentic Media, 2004

Reaction Reaction Reaction Reaction

CIRCLE:

TICK:

Total rubbish ☐   Not sure ☐   Worth thinking about ☐   Genius ☐

FILL:

....
....
....
....

Name: **Karis Breegan**

Age: **21**

Town: **Stockport**

Occupation: **Hairdresser**

Passions: **Music**

Better invention: scissors or electricity?

Scissors.

Most embarrassing moment?

I had to be sick once while I was cutting someone's hair! Luckily, though, I made it into the toilet first.

Who do you trust to cut your hair?

Sophia – one of my colleagues.

Favourite song of all time?

'Don't Go' by Yazoo.

When you were a kid what did you want to be when you grew up?

Hairdresser!

How many countries have you visited?

Four or five.

Do you have any interesting hobbies?

Just going out and having a good time.

Have you ever had to forgive anybody?

Yes. It was difficult.

What would you say to someone who's finding it difficult to forgive one of their friends?

Don't live in the past. Get over it and move on.

THE FATHER
– TOTAL FORGIVENESS AND RESTORED RELATIONSHIP

Just like Sally, we may well find saying sorry the hardest thing to do, but we will always be so glad we made up our mind to do so. We may try to build up long explanations or rambling apologies, but it is unnecessary. Every one of us, when in our desperation we turn to God, gets the same reception. In his mercy he accepts us and loves us. We don't understand why because we know that humanly speaking his forgiveness is not deserved. But we are so grateful that he does this.

T his is why the parable could also be called the Parable of the Prodigal Father. Our heavenly Father is 'prodigal' in terms of the lavish, unrestrained and totally undeserved generosity that he pours down on us. When Sally's dad saw her at the end of the station he did not care about his dignity. **THIS WAS NOT ABOUT HIS REPUTATION: IT WAS ABOUT HIS UNCONDITIONAL LOVE.** He must have been thinking constantly about what his daughter might have gone through while she had been away. Just one look would have confirmed his worst fears. But perhaps because he could see that Sally had sunk to the very bottom, he knew he had to let her know that she could be fully restored. This is love in abundance. It is extravagant. It feels out of this world – because that's exactly what it is.

When we return to our beloved heavenly Father, the embrace we receive is not just a sign of our forgiveness; it is more a sign of our restored relationship. It is our Father who takes the initiative. We may be trying to stammer out our apologies but he is no longer listening. He is simply too excited that his precious child has come back home. Sally's dad shows everyone present that the relationship is fully restored when he gives her the family heirloom – the ring that had been handed down through the generations. Amazingly this restoration takes place before Sally had time to prove she is truly sorry – and so it is in our own experience. Simply acknowledging that we are unworthy is what allows God's unconditional love to flow.

It is wonderful to recognize that however far we have wandered away, whatever possessions we have squandered, however immoral the life we've led, our Father is scouring the horizon for us, waiting for us to appear in the distance. Despite our mess he will know us in an instant. He will know the way we look, the way we walk and how we are thinking. His eyes will fill with tears, but this time they will be tears of joy, not the tears of pain he has shed as we have gone down our own treacherous paths. And when we return, there is no questioning, no inquisition 'just to be sure' of our motivation, no standing down, no quarantine period and no condemnation: just the fullness of our Father's love.

Keith Tondeur, *Street Parables for Today*, Authentic Media, 2004

ReactionReactionReactionReaction

CIRCLE:

😊 😟 😐 😮 😌 😲

TICK:

Total rubbish ☐   Not sure ☐   Worth thinking about ☐   Genius ☐

FILL:

....

....

Hidden pearls

There are people that don't please me but
I have to love them in the Lord even though
I may not like them much the way they are. Just
a clash of personalities, but you forgive them
because the Bible tells us to.

God Did It, So Why Can't You?

Helen talks

Ever been told that you are your own worst critic? So often we find it even harder to forgive ourselves than to forgive other people. We can have grace for other people, we can be merciful, but to ourselves it's another story. Do you ever say things to yourself that you would never dream of saying to anyone else? Once I caught myself really laying into myself in my head about how stupid I was not to take an opportunity that had presented itself. I was telling myself off for not being more confident and not taking risks. Suddenly I stopped and thought about what I was saying. I realized that I wouldn't dream of speaking to my worst enemy in the way I was speaking to myself!

It is good to have high standards and to push yourself to get better and to be holy and more like Jesus but the balance to that is that we need to learn to forgive ourselves when we mess up. If we hang on to bitterness and unforgiveness towards ourselves we are making a mockery of what God did for us on the cross. It's like saying, 'Jesus, I know you died for me, but I'm sorry that just isn't quite good enough. I am so bad that even your death can't deal with what I've done.' THAT IS ACTUALLY BEING RUDE AND DISOBEDIENT TO GOD! Sometimes we just need to read what God says about us in the Bible and believe it. Galatians 2:19–20 says, 'It was the law itself that caused me to end my life under the law. I died to the law so that I could live for God. I have been nailed to the cross with Christ. So I am not the one living now – it is Christ living in me. I still live in my body, but I live by faith in the Son of God. He is the one who loved me and gave himself to save me.' His death has saved us, it has put to death all the wrong things we have done. We need to believe it and live in it and forgive ourselves, otherwise we are actually walking in unbelief and disobedience to God. So once you have repented and asked for God's forgiveness for something, don't let it drag you down any more. Enjoy living in the extravagant freedom that Christ has given us.

ReactionReactionReactionReaction

CIRCLE:

😊 🙁 😐 😯 🙃 😮

TICK:

Total rubbish ☐ Not sure ☐ Worth thinking about ☐ Genius ☐

FILL:

....

....

....

....

Hidden pearls

Norma and I have never gone to sleep without
things being 100% between us. We sort
everything out first, forgive each other and
put it right. But we're too old to fight now!

Head to the beach and take some time out to do the following exercise and learn more about forgiveness in action.

A Walk in the DESERT

How did you get here? Replay your journey in your mind, consciously leaving behind all the things you need to do, the people you need to speak to, the expectations that others have of you.

A t the start of his ministry Jesus spent 40 days in the wilderness, alone. At other times he spent nights on a mountain in prayer, talking to his Father.

This is your time – this is your desert. This is your space to be with God, and God is here. Breathe deeply – enjoy the space.

Take off your shoes and socks and walk in the sand. Look at the footprints you have made.

THINK BACK OVER THIS LAST WEEK – WHAT FOOTPRINTS HAVE YOU LEFT BEHIND YOU? What impression have you left on the people you have met? Have you trampled on anyone, put anyone down? Do you need to ask for forgiveness? Write a prayer to God on a piece of paper.

Walk in the sand again, putting your feet in exactly the same places that you walked before.

Think back over this last week – have you followed Jesus? Have you gone where he has led you, or chosen your own path? Do you need to ask for forgiveness? Add this to your prayer.

Now roll the paper up and, as you hold it, ask for God's forgiveness. Leave the paper buried in the centre of the sand.

Deserts are dry, dusty places. Think about the areas of your life where you feel dry and in need of God's Spirit. Write these in the sand in front of you with your finger – just for you and God to see. When you have finished, smooth the sand again for the people who will come after you.

Read Isaiah 35:1–7. God promises streams of water in the desert. He promises forgiveness and joy to those who ask for it. Drink some cool water and receive God's forgiveness.

Stay and enjoy God's presence.

When it's time to go, put some sand in your pockets to remind you of meeting God here.

Jenny Baker, *Transforming Prayer*, **Spring Harvest Publishing and Authentic Media, 2004**

ReactionReactionReactionReaction

CIRCLE:

TICK:

Total rubbish ☐   Not sure ☐   Worth thinking about ☐   Genius ☐

FILL:

....

....

....

....

ELEPHANTINE Forgiveness

Read Matthew 18:21–35

THE PHRASE 'FORGIVE AND FORGET' IS NOT IN THE BIBLE. There is plenty of forgiving going on, but forgetting is not once listed in its vicinity. In fact, I think that phrase undermines the cost and central thrust of forgiveness. Amos 8:7 says, 'The LORD made a promise. He used his name, "Pride of Jacob", and made this promise: "I will never forget what those people did."' Forgiveness is not a casual thing. It cost Jesus his life to provide it for us. Hebrews 9:22 says, 'The law says that almost everything must be made clean by blood. Sins cannot be forgiven without a blood sacrifice.'

Forgiveness is not about saying, 'Oh, that's all right, it wasn't that hurtful, you're fine.' It's about saying, 'Yes, that wasn't good. It hurt me. But I have freely received forgiveness, so I am going to "give it on" to you.' That literally is forgiving. Giving on what you have received.

There is an episode of *The Simpsons* where Marge is in prison and, for handiness, instead of tidying up properly, Bart and Lisa quite literally sweep everything under the carpet. At the outset it works, but eventually they are surfing across their living room on a tide of trash. We often employ this handy option to keep the peace, but if you ignore what it is that has hurt, it prevents the power of the cross coming to bear on it. Little things that people say or do gradually accumulate until relationships suffer crisis moments. We've never addressed the issues, often with our closest friends and family, because **WE'VE CONFUSED FORGIVING WITH IGNORING**. I recently experienced this in a situation where someone had been annoying me more and more over a period of months. I thought I was so impressively restrained in staying quiet on the subject, but then one day, a straw broke this camel's back and I exploded into an unpleasant contorted version of myself. Are there some folks who you need to 'forgive from the heart', not just the head? This will involve privately letting go to God, but sometimes will mean contacting them. In any conversations that ensue, you may well discover that you need to ask their forgiveness too.

Pray for the grace and the boldness to confront and forgive. Too often we just do one or the other.

Andy Flannagan, *God 360°*, Spring Harvest Publishing and Authentic Media, 2006

ReactionReactionReactionReaction

CIRCLE:

😊 😦 😐 😲 😕 😮

TICK:

Total rubbish ☐ Not sure ☐ Worth thinking about ☐ Genius ☐

FILL:

....

....

....

....

FREEDOM

Helen talks

Forgiving others is something we all know we should do. It's in the Bible and Jesus was really good at it. I sometimes find it easier to forgive big things than little things. Let me explain. When someone broke into our car last year and stole our CD player it was really annoying, it cost us time and money that we didn't have, but I found it quite easy to forgive the person who stole it. Instead of spending the last year on a one-woman vendetta against car thieves, prowling the streets trying to find out who did it, I prayed to God and said that I forgave that person and moved on. Case closed. However, I think it's much harder to forgive people for the ongoing little things they do to make our lives difficult.

When I was in college there was someone on the course with me who absolutely got on my last nerve. It wasn't even as if he'd done anything particular to hurt me or upset me but I just found him really, really annoying. Let's call him Frank (that's not his real name by the way). The way he talked, the things he said to me, the way he reacted, the things he did just got me really wound up and offended. I remember one day standing in a queue to get food behind Frank, seething as usual at some annoying thing he had just done. Suddenly it dawned on me. Hang on a minute, who is this hurting? Here I am, all churned up inside, stressed out and annoyed, and **FRANK IS COMPLETELY OBLIVIOUS!** I haven't even told him how I feel; he doesn't even know. So all this time I am the one getting stressed and annoyed and what effect is that having on him? None! I am the one bursting a blood vessel and probably getting an ulcer, while he floats through life unaware.

From that point I realized I had to do one of two things. Either, tell Frank the problem, forgive him and move on, or, not tell him and just forgive him and move on. Notice the common theme in both of these options? I decided that in this situation it probably wouldn't be helpful to tell him how difficult I found him, but I decided to make a conscious effort to forgive him for all the things he did that wound me up. Oh my goodness, what a difference it made! Seriously, by letting it go and just forgiving him I was able to relax and accept Frank. When something happened that would have previously wound me up I would just give it to God and let it go. I don't think it made much difference to him, but it made a huge difference to me. One of my friends even suggested that whenever Frank annoyed me or did something to upset me I should pray for God's blessing on him and thank God for him. Through doing this I found that I was actually able to start appreciating things about him. Instead of being annoyed by Frank's rude and blunt way of communicating, I thanked God for his honesty and actually ended up appreciating this about him.

So give it a go. Maybe you have been really seriously wronged by someone, maybe they don't deserve your forgiveness, maybe they even laugh at the pain they have caused you. The same principle applies. **THE ANGER AND BITTERNESS YOU FEEL TOWARDS THEM DOESN'T HURT THEM, IT HURTS YOU**. It actually lets them continue hurting you after whatever they originally did is long over. By forgiving them you release yourself from their hold. If you choose to forgive, no matter what, it isn't letting them off the hook, it's letting you off the hook, it's allowing you to move on with your life. I know my story is a light-hearted one and I know many of you will have had things done to you that are really hard to forgive but please let God help you and release you from these things. If you need help talking through things and forgiving, then please find an older Christian you can trust. Talk to them and get them to pray with you about how you feel, then stay accountable so that you keep forgiving.

ReactionReactionReactionReaction

CIRCLE:

😊 🙁 😐 😦 😌 😮

TICK:

Total rubbish ☐   Not sure ☐   Worth thinking about ☐   Genius ☐

FILL:

....

....

....

....

Beginning to Forgive

Why should we try to forgive people who hurt us? What if they are not even sorry?

You may think that, humanly speaking, those who abuse others don't deserve to be forgiven. It is certainly a very difficult thing to get your head around. Some people who have been abused feel that forgiveness is impossible. I honestly believe that it has been part of my healing process.

I had to forgive every person who had harmed me. I worked through it with a lady I trusted. I wrote the names of every person and literally asked God to take away my anger, resentment, bitterness and hurt. I asked him to heal me of anything that would cause me to hurt others. I gave him each name in turn and asked him to take the pain and trauma out of the memories. Then I asked him not to count their sin against them. I asked him to have mercy on them and change them into people who honoured him. Of those people that I am still aware of, or hear about from time to time, I have begun to see God answering those prayers. – Ems.

True forgiveness will take a long time, so the sooner we start to work on it, the sooner we can start to get on with our lives again. Bitterness is the worst burden to carry and is both self-destructive and pointless. It will not help you and may well stop you from being healed of any hurt. Make a decision to try and get rid of it the minute you see it in yourself.

What amazed me when I first thought about it, was the realization that people who had hurt me could be forgiven, not just by me but by God, too. No one is unforgivable. No matter what they may have done. I know this sort of thing is hard. It doesn't mean letting them get away with it. Some people may need and deserve to be punished in some way. But that may well not be up to you. You have the choice of whether to forgive them or to hold on to what they have done. Forgiveness, genuine forgiveness is tough but, believe me, it's way better than the alternatives. I have met so many people who have had less abuse than me that have been totally eaten up inside, incapable of having any sort of normal relationship with males or females. I can't take any credit for my healing. God is my healer and he can be yours too. – Ems

Self-pity is totally understandable but it is not a long-term or healthy solution. It may be as far as we can get without God and loving friends to help us through. When we pity our own situation we tend to wallow in it, reminding ourselves over and over of the same things. Self-pity can exaggerate or exacerbate the problem and leave us feeling so helpless and hopeless that we end up not doing anything about it. Be careful to watch out that your sadness is well channelled. Bitterness can be disguised as self-pity very quickly.

Ems Hancock and Ian Henderson, *Sorted?*, Spring Harvest Publishing and Authentic Media, 2006

ReactionReactionReactionReaction

CIRCLE:

☺ ☹ 😐 😲 🙂 😮

TICK:

Total rubbish ☐   Not sure ☐   Worth thinking about ☐   Genius ☐

FILL:

....
....
....
....

Reality Check

DEAR . . .

Back in the olden days before mobile phones, email, Twitter and Facebook, people used to write letters! You can ask your parents about it if you want, or maybe even your grandparents. Letters used to be the only way you could get in touch with a friend or relative, other than hopping on your horse and riding over to see them. Letters take time to write and, back in those days, people would spend ages hand writing just the right thing to communicate to each other. Now we can drop someone a text or an email in a matter of seconds and often we don't give it much thought. For this Reality Check we want you to write two letters, so sit yourself down, find a pen you like and collect your thoughts.

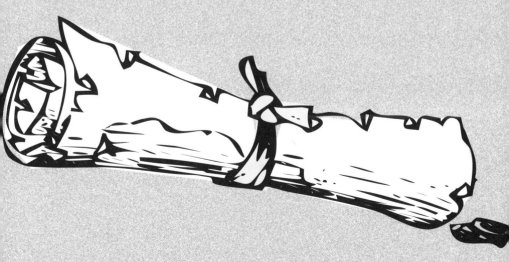

...YOU ARE FORGIVEN

This is a letter from God to you. Think about something you have asked God for forgiveness for and write a letter from him to you telling you that you are forgiven. Think of some of the verses you have read about how he completely forgives you and accepts you. Use your imagination.

Date: Today

Address: God's Throne, The Golden Throne Room, God's Palace, Heaven, Eternity

Dear (add your name), ...

. . . .

. . . .

. . . .

. . . .

. . . .

. . . .

. . . .

. . . .

I love you so much,

Yours forever,

God

We hope you enjoyed that, now here is something that might be a bit trickier. Think about something you need to forgive someone else for. It might be big or small, it could be something from years ago or something that happened yesterday. You might even want to write it to God, if you feel bitter towards him about something that has happened to you. Think about how much God has forgiven you and then write a letter forgiving that person for what they have done. It might be something they don't even know they have done. If it is, explain what happened and how it made you feel.

Date: . . . .

Their address (if you know it)

. . . .

. . . .

. . . .

Dear (fill in their name), ...

. . . .

. . . .

. . . .

. . . .

. . . .

. . . .

. . . .

. . . .

. . . .

. . . .

. . . .

Thanks for listening,

. . . .

Now you've finished, think about what you want to do with this letter. Sometimes just writing down how you feel can help you really forgive someone in your heart. However, now that you have thought through how you feel it might be helpful to call or visit the person and tell them what you have written. Or you could send this letter to them in the post. It's up to you.

Eternal Life

And we know that the Son of God has come and has given us understanding. So now we can know the one who is true, and we live in that true God. We are in his Son, Jesus Christ. He is the true God, and he is eternal life.

(1 John 5:20)

First up

For some people this life is all they believe there is. They think they will live their 80 years on earth, have good times, bad times, make money, lose money, meet people, lose people, and at the end that will be it. They think it's as simple as that. No higher plan, nothing spiritual going on, nothing after death, just emptiness.

As a Christian you might be thinking a bit differently; you might think that eternal life is there for you after you die. You might think that after death you go on to either live with God, or without God eternally. But have you ever considered that eternal life might be available before you die? Look at the verse at the start of this Life Lesson. It says Jesus is God and eternal life. Eh? Get your head round that if you can! The Bible talks a lot about eternal life being available now and later. In this Life Lesson we are going to look at what it is and how you can start living it right now.

DEAD END

ETERNAL LIFE – Question Time

Chip talks

What is eternal life?

That's a very big topic! I think the best, most concise answer can be found in Jesus' prayer just before he's taken away to be crucified. He says:

> And this is eternal life: that people can know you, the only true God, and that they can know Jesus Christ, the one you sent.

(John 17:3)

So basically, when we begin to know Jesus we begin to experience eternal life. That's what the Bible says.

When does it start?

A lot of people think that eternal life only begins once you die, but based on this verse that just isn't true. **DO YOU HAVE TO WAIT UNTIL YOU DIE TO GET TO KNOW GOD? NO.** There are millions of people who already have a friendship with him right now. They're talking with him, reading his promises to them in the Bible and putting his words into action every day. By spending time getting to know God, they've already begun to have eternal life.

What about after you die?

It just keeps getting better, really. Apostle Paul puts it like this:

> Now we see God as if we are looking at a reflection in a mirror. But then, in the future, we will see him right before our eyes. Now I know only a part, but at that time I will know fully, as God has known me.

(1 Corinthians 13:12)

So there's definitely a deeper level of knowing God reserved for once you die on earth. That must mean that eternal life gets better too!

But wouldn't that get boring after a while?

I know, at first it looks that way. But ask anyone mature enough in their faith, and they'll tell you that their relationship with Jesus just gets better with time. It's not like a job, where the excitement wears off after a while.

'No one has ever seen, no one has ever heard, no one has ever imagined what God has prepared for those who love him.'

(Isaiah 64:4, 1 Corinthians 2:9)

See? It's literally mind-blowing.

Who gives us eternal life?

It comes from God, obviously. But more specifically, **IT'S THE HOLY SPIRIT THAT PRODUCES ETERNAL LIFE IN US**.

If you live to satisfy your sinful self, the harvest you will get from that will be eternal death. But if you live to please the Spirit, your harvest from the Spirit will be eternal life. We must not get tired of doing good. We will receive our harvest of eternal life at the right time. We must not give up.

(Galatians 6:8–9)

So, it's kind of a two-way thing between us and the Spirit, and we have to persevere at times.

ReactionReactionReactionReaction

CIRCLE:

😊 ☹️ 😐 😦 😕 😮

TICK:

Total rubbish ☐   Not sure ☐   Worth thinking about ☐   Genius ☐

FILL:

....
....
....
....

Name: **Sam Rankin**

Age: **14**

Town: **Sale, Manchester**

Passionate about: **Music and football**

What football team do you support?

Liverpool.

What has been your favourite moment in life so far?

I will get back to you.

Which bands are you into at the moment?

Dream Theatre, Opeth, Symphony X, and just progressive music in general.

What do you hate most about girls?

The way they go behind each others' backs and stuff like that.

Where is heaven?

Well, I don't really know what to say . . . It's said to be up in the sky but who knows?

How do you get to heaven?

By living the life that God wants you to lead.

What advice would you give to someone who thought they were going to heaven but wasn't sure?

Read the Bible. Find out from someone who's a Christian what you should be doing to get to heaven.

Fear of DEATH

Helen Talks

Are you scared of dying? Some people seem to go through life without any fear of death at all, loving the adrenaline rush of doing something dangerous. They climb huge mountains, raft dangerous rivers, jump out of planes, and do crazy stuff like base jumping or free running. For them, the rush and the experience, or the potential achievement of a goal outweighs the risks; they would rather risk death than have a safe, 'boring' life.

For other people, fear of death guides and restricts them every day. They go through life continually assessing possible dangers so they can avoid them. They don't take risks and they avoid any situation where they are unsure of or not in control of the outcome. They avoid danger at every turn. Other people may have come close to death, perhaps through an accident or illness and they live in constant fear of the same thing happening again.

I don't know where you are on the spectrum between these two extremes, but as Christians we don't need to fear death. Read through the following verses, taken from Revelation 21:1–6:

> Then I saw a new heaven and a new earth. The first heaven and the first earth had disappeared. Now there was no sea. And I saw the holy city, the new Jerusalem, coming down out of heaven from God. It was prepared like a bride dressed for her husband. I heard a loud voice from the throne. It said, 'Now God's home is with people. He will live with them. They will be his people. God himself will be with them and will be their God. He will wipe away every tear from their eyes. There will be no more death, sadness, crying or pain. All the old ways are gone.'

> The one who was sitting on the throne said, 'Look, I am making everything new!' Then he said, 'Write this, because these words are true and can be trusted.'

> The one on the throne said to me, 'It is finished! I am the Alpha and the Omega, the Beginning and the End. I will give free water from the spring of the water of life to anyone who is thirsty.'

And check out these verses from 1 Corinthians 15:12–23:

We tell everyone that Christ was raised from death. So why do some of you say that people will not be raised from death? If no one will ever be raised from death, then Christ has never been raised. And if Christ has never been raised, then the message we tell is worth nothing. And your faith is worth nothing. And we will also be guilty of lying about God, because we have told people about him, saying that he raised Christ from death. And if no one is raised from death, then God never raised Christ from death. If those who have died are not raised, then Christ has not been raised either. And if Christ has not been raised from death, then your faith is for nothing; you are still guilty of your sins. And those in Christ who have already died are lost. If our hope in Christ is only for this life here on earth, then people should feel more sorry for us than for anyone else.

But Christ really has been raised from death – the first one
of all those who will be raised. Death comes to people because
of what one man did. But now there is resurrection from death
because of another man. I mean that in Adam all of us die.
And in the same way, in Christ all of us will be made alive
again. But everyone will be raised to life in the right order.
Christ was first to be raised. Then, when Christ comes again,
those who belong to him will be raised to life.

Write down how you feel about dying. Do these verses change how you feel?

....
....
....
....
....
....
....

ReactionReactionReactionReaction

CIRCLE:

TICK:

Total rubbish ☐   Not sure ☐   Worth thinking about ☐   Genius ☐

FILL:

....
....
....
....

Eternal Life

Now or Later?

When we limit the kingdom of God to the future tense, we deny its very existence. It must either be present in all times or in none at all. That means, of course, that the kingdom must exist here and now on this earth, as broken as it is. God has established this world as an integral part of his divine order. The fact that his creatures have rejected his perfect kingdom has left the King unperturbed; his kingship will prevail.

Through his Son, God has answered the cry of a regretful people and established his new order on the earth. On the cross, Christ has been crowned King of the world and in his resurrected life he has begun to redress the balance. The world is being remade and, as new creations, we experience this at first hand. Eternal life has come early and ahead of judgement day. **FROM THIS DAY FORTH, THE WORLD'S FUTURE CAN BE EXPERIENCED BY ANYONE WHO WANTS IT, NOT AS A PREDICTION BUT AS A FULFILLED PROMISE.** All the things that are beyond fallen humanity such as forgiveness, healing, wholeness, purity and eternal life have been made available by the King. Everything that man has lost can be regained. The subjects of the kingdom are caught up and irrevocably changed as God's eternity has become their reality and God's plans have become their path. To live in the kingdom is to live simultaneously in the past, present and future; to be part of the story of creation. In this sense, the subjects of the kingdom are more important than the United Nations. It is they who know how the world should be and they that have grasped that vision ahead of time. It is they who know the outcome of history and the hope of the world.

Yet, the kingdom is not just in conflict with our timetable; it is in conflict with everything that we know as human beings. The kingdom, by its very nature, never quite fits into our broken world. It is there to disturb us; to point out that it wasn't meant to be this way. The kingdom can't be grasped by a human mind, but instead seeks to shape it. The kingdom can't be crammed into human history, but rather absorbs it. **THE KINGDOM IS BEYOND HUMANITY, BEYOND INTELLECT, BEYOND MORALITY, BEYOND POLITICS, BEYOND THE CHURCH, BEYOND YESTERDAY, TODAY AND TOMORROW.** It is God's plan for all human existence, and for that matter, all animal, vegetable and mineral existence. To this end, it is not about where the kingdom fits into our world but where our world fits into the kingdom.

So when is the kingdom coming? Simple: it has come, it is coming and it will come. It is both now and not yet. It is both imminent and immanent. This world is part of the story of God's kingdom, and while the story is not complete, it is more than begun. And it is ours, both now and forever.

Russell Rook and Aaron White, *The Hitchhiker's Guide to the Kingdom*, **Spring Harvest Publishing and Authentic Media, 2007**

ReactionReactionReactionReaction

CIRCLE:

TICK:

Total rubbish ☐   Not sure ☐   Worth thinking about ☐   Genius ☐

FILL:

....
....
....
....

Heaven Goggles

Chip talks

To be honest, most of the decisions I make in a typical day are about temporary things. What time shall I set the alarm for? Which cereal shall I eat? How hot do I want my shower to be? Which clothes do I wear? And that's all before I've even left the house in the morning. But then as the day moves on there are bigger, more important decisions to make as well. Where will I find the motivation I need for this or that task? Who will I spend time talking to? How will I accomplish the things I need to get done in the time that I've got available to do them?

If I'm not careful, I can begin to treat temporary things as more important than what's eternal. My immediate needs and desires receive more attention than those things that really matter. I may not feel like spending an extra 15 minutes in conversation with someone who's having a really tough time, but in light of eternity that may be the most important 15 minutes I ever spend with that person.

Think of it like this. What if you were able to put on 'heaven goggles'? You'd be able to see everything around you – the people, the opportunities, even yourself – in light of eternity. Suddenly your priorities would shift to the things that are really important. All of the temporary stuff that takes up so much of your attention would begin to fade into insignificance once you'd seen the world from this point of view. Jesus said that he did nothing without first seeing his Father in heaven do it (John 5:19). He understood this concept perfectly, and he encourages us to do the same.

Prayer:

Lord Jesus, please help me to have your view of the world around me today. Help me to see those opportunities where I can make a difference in eternity. I trust you to lead me and use me to be a bright light, even in the darkest of places. Amen.

Further reading:

- *Matthew 6:19–20*
- *Mark 10:28–30*
- *Ephesians 2:10*
- *Colossians 3:1–2*

ReactionReactionReactionReaction

CIRCLE:

☺ ☹ 😐 ❗ 😕 😮

TICK:

Total rubbish ☐   Not sure ☐   Worth thinking about ☐   Genius ☐

FILL:

....
....
....

The Good TEST

Helen Talks

There's a preacher/evangelist from New Zealand called Ray Comfort who goes out on the streets doing something he calls 'The Good Test'. He asks people if they think they're good enough to go to heaven when they die, and 99% of the time they say, 'Yes'. He then goes on to ask them why, and they explain that they are a good person, they've never killed anyone and they've always tried to help others, so why shouldn't they go to heaven?

The evangelist then goes on to ask, 'Have you ever told a lie?'

They respond, 'Yes'.

'Have you ever taken the Lord's name in vain?'

'Yes,' they respond again.

'Have you ever coveted something that wasn't yours, or had lustful feelings towards someone you weren't married to?'

With a snigger they usually answer, 'Yes'.

Ray then summarizes: 'So, you're a self-confessed lying, blaspheming, covetous, adulterer at heart! Why should God let you into heaven?'

Harsh! But the point he is making is that **NONE OF US CAN POSSIBLY BE JUDGED 'GOOD' IF WE ARE MEASURED BY GOD'S PERFECT STANDARD.** Jesus himself said that ultimately only God is good. Even the best of us will fall short. The only way we can be made good is by trusting in Jesus and what he did for us on the cross. If we make him our Master and Saviour, then his sacrifice makes us clean. Despite our sinful nature, we can say we are good enough for God and good enough for heaven because of what Jesus did, not because of something we've done for ourselves.

Most other religions teach people they must work to earn forgiveness and eternal life in heaven. They must do certain things, say certain prayers, go on pilgrimages and whatever else. After all, wouldn't it be easier to at least try and attain perfection, rather than accept the fact that we can't actually do anything good enough to justify ourselves? We often prefer to be able to fix things or make them right on our own. God's grace says, 'No! You can't add anything to what Jesus did on the cross by your actions.' He said it himself, 'It is FINISHED.' Our response should be simply to live lives of gratitude to God, joyfully serving him and following his ways, because we know he has the best possible plan for us.

Do you find it hard to believe God would forgive you for certain things? If so, list some of those things here:

....

....

Now spend some time praying, receiving God's total forgiveness and thanking him for it.

Further reading:

• *John 3:16*

• *2 Corinthians 5:16–18*

ReactionReactionReactionReaction

CIRCLE:

☺ ☹ 😐 😦 😌 😲

TICK:

Total rubbish ☐   Not sure ☐   Worth thinking about ☐   Genius ☐

FILL:

....

....

Read Ecclesiastes chapter 3.

Ｔhere is one week of my school experience that I will never forget. A lovely young guy called Phillip Johnston was killed in a bicycle accident. For many of the pupils, it was our first encounter with the frailty of life. The headmaster wisely allowed us all to go to the funeral, and you could feel five hundred young heads and hearts trying to process this strange new information.

Later that week we were scheduled to perform a concert for many of the local pensioners. There was a strong accent on comedy, and a group of us were performing 'Summer Nights' from *Grease*, with a twist – the girls were in leather jackets and denim, and the boys were in . . . well you get the picture. In light of the recent events, it all felt a bit strange, and we wondered about not going ahead with the routine. However, we did go ahead and, as ever, the old folks loved it.

A few days later I was wandering around the imposing cathedral of St Patrick in Armargh, and there was a massive Bible sitting open at Ecclesiastes chapter 3. The words jumped out at me:

There is a time to cry and a time to laugh.
There is a time to be sad and a time to dance with joy.

Something of the reality of life was planted in me that week, and more importantly, the truth that God knew and understood. Reading those verses it was as if I heard him saying, 'I know, I know. But it won't always be this way.'

Are there specific periods of your life that you could reference to some of the phrases?

Write a paragraph about those times, exploring how you felt, and why. But also write some notes about that phrase's 'opposite'.

There is a rhythm here, that speaks of the changing seasons of life. Whoever promised us that we would live in eternal summer? Thank God for the varying seasons of your life.

Andy Flannagan, *God 360°*, Spring Harvest Publishing and Authentic Media, 2006

ReactionReactionReactionReaction

CIRCLE:

FILL:

TICK:

Total rubbish ☐ Not sure ☐ Worth thinking about ☐ Genius ☐

FILL:

....

....

....

....

Heaven and Hell

Then Jacob woke up and said, 'I know that the LORD is in this place, but I did not know he was here until I slept.' Jacob was afraid and said, 'This is a very great place. This is the house of God. This is the gate to heaven.'

(Genesis 28:16–17)

5

First up

Picture it. After a long and happy life, finally your time is up. You slip into an endless sleep and awake to the sight of a bright light. You walk forward to see tall pearly gates, a man in a long flowing robe and silver-white hair greets you and, after checking your name off on an old fashioned scroll, motions you to enter the gates. As your feet bounce along on the lighter-than-air grass you see children laughing, hear harps playing and see little lambs frolicking amongst the flowers. You take a seat on a cloud and are instantly whisked away to meet God, a kindly old man with a long flowing white beard and loving eyes.

Is this your picture of heaven?

Or picture this. After a long and happy life, finally your time is up. You slip into an endless sleep and awake to the sight of a dingy red light. You peer through the semi-darkness and see flames and smoke licking through a charred iron gateway. As you advance you spot a man dressed from head to foot in red lycra, two pointy horns peeping from the top of his head and a sharp pitchfork in his right hand. You turn to try and get back to where you came from, but it's too late, he's got you and you are dragged, screaming into the red darkness.

Is this your picture of hell?

Our culture has painted some fairly stereotypical pictures of heaven and hell for us. You'd be surprised how much of what we think actually has nothing to do with what the Bible says and is just myth and legend. We know that the Bible speaks of both a heaven and a hell. A place where there is communion with God and a place of eternal separation from God. It mentions angels and demons and a God of truth and a devil who is the father of lies. Whether God has a white beard and the devil is red and carries a pitchfork is really a bit irrelevant. Take some time out to research what the Bible really says and sort out the myth from the truth.

Is Heaven Your Home?

Helen talks

'If God exists, then why would he send people to hell if he is so loving?'

It's a question we've been asked loads of times in schools across the UK. People just can't get their heads round how a loving God could send people to hell – a place of forever suffering. Why does God make it so hard? Is he just some cruel tyrant who wants people to suffer?

We believe that God is loving but also that he is just. He is a God of justice, a fair God. **HE SENT JESUS SO THAT WE DON'T HAVE TO GO TO HELL BUT HE WON'T FORCE ANYONE TO LOVE HIM OR BELIEVE IN HIM.** He designed us with the inbuilt ability to choose to walk away from him, ignore him and not love him. And many people do just that. God wants them in heaven but they choose to walk away from him.

We know that heaven is a place where you can worship God freely and where you get to be in his presence. For people who don't know God or want to know him that would not be much fun! That's why the idea of hell has become a bit glamorized in today's society. People don't like the idea of hanging out with God, praising him and spending time with him in heaven.

It's our job as Christians to pray for our friends and to talk to them about Jesus, to show them how much he loves them and what an amazing life we can have with him. Also, we've got to remember, **AS CHRISTIANS WE ARE NOT AT HOME HERE ON EARTH. HEAVEN IS OUR HOME – THIS IS THE JOURNEY TO GET THERE, THE DREAM BEFORE WE WAKE UP**. The Bible says, 'Dear friends, you are like foreigners and strangers in this world. So I beg you to keep your lives free from the evil things you want to do, those desires that fight against your true selves' (1 Peter 2:11). Let's not get too settled in here!

ReactionReactionReactionReaction

CIRCLE:

TICK:

Total rubbish ☐   Not sure ☐   Worth thinking about ☐   Genius ☐

FILL:

....

....

....

....

Judgement

Jesus is quite clear about who is the Judge of time and history. This job belongs to the one perfect King who has overseen everything from the beginning. He will decide which disciples are true, and which are false. He will make the necessary, just and perfect judgements. I find this challenging as deep down I believe that I would, and do, make a very good judge. I find it easy to judge my fellow believers and my fellow man . . . Only God can say whether someone is in or out of the kingdom. Only God, thank God, can make the final judgement on someone's life. No instant video replay needed here. The where, the how, the why, the what, the when and the who of the kingdom all belong to God.

I once went fishing on a pier overnight. We were fishing for sand trout and Spanish mackerel, or so I was led to believe. I am not a great fisherman, and I spent most of the time trying to stick live, wriggling shrimps onto my hook, flailing my line into the water, slowly reeling it back in, discovering that my bait had been stolen by criminal denizens of the deep and watching everyone else haul in loads of monster-sized, succulent fish. We were out there for a long time, and still I had no joy in the catching department. The person who had accompanied me on my fishing excursion had long since given up, and had gone back to the car for a nap. But I was determined; **I WOULD NOT LEAVE THAT PIER WITHOUT HOOKING A FISH.** My line was constantly getting snagged on seaweed and rocks, and it was a struggle to bring it back to the surface. At one point I felt I had snagged a particularly nasty rock, and was really working to get free. I suddenly realized that the rock was fighting back. It was a fish! I reeled that line as hard as I could, and in my excitement to bring the fish up fast, I actually managed to impale it on the end of my rod.

So there I was, standing on the pier like a complete dunce, holding a long rod with a fish attached to the top like a smelly, writhing weathervane. I brought the rod and fish down to the ground, and thought very seriously about touching the still-squirming beast. It was gasping, and actually making a noise, sort of like a low, wet grunting, only somehow worse. It also very clearly had teeth. I was at a complete loss. Finally a young girl came along, saw my predicament, and expertly removed the fish. She looked at it carefully and said: 'It's too small, no good, you want to keep it.' It would have been extremely difficult for me to have made that judgement by myself, having no frame of reference for the proper size or merits of fish. It took an expert to tell me whether or not the fish was a keeper. I did not want to throw the fish back: it was mine, I had caught it, it was special to me. But it was the appropriate thing to do.

I would feel uncomfortable making the comparison between my silly fishing trip and the divine judgement at the end of the world, if Jesus hadn't said something very much like it already in the parable of the dragnet. Jesus is the expert judge, not us. And humans are far more precious to him than my fish was to me. He does not want to throw anyone back, but he has to be true to his nature, which is completely just. A good friend of mine likes to say to people, 'You know, if it was up to me, you'd be getting into heaven, and I probably wouldn't. I THINK YOU'RE A GREAT PERSON, AND I KNOW HOW SINFUL I AM. BUT I'M NOT THE JUDGE, GOD IS. AND HE KNOWS WAY BETTER THAN ME.'

Russell Rook and Aaron White, *The Hitchhiker's Guide to the Kingdom*, Spring Harvest Publishing and Authentic Media, 2007

ReactionReactionReactionReaction

CIRCLE:

😊 🙁 😐 😮 😕 😲

TICK:

Total rubbish ☐   Not sure ☐   Worth thinking about ☐   Genius ☐

FILL:

....

....

....

....

Hidden pearls

The Bible makes it clear that heaven is a wonderful place, something that we've never experienced. It's difficult to imagine something as marvellous as that. When you're old and you've got aches and pains, you do look forward to getting rid of all that.

HEAVEN

chipK's mind

Have you ever wondered what heaven will be like? You know you have. I always ask myself stuff like: 'Will I be able to fly in heaven?' or 'What will we spend all our time doing up there?' or 'What's it going to look like, especially compared to all the beauty we already have down here on earth?'

O n a recent trip to the States, Helen and I experienced a taste of heaven when we visited a well-known Christian University. Our mouths literally dropped open the moment we stepped in to the main reception. **EVER HEARD THE PHRASE, 'I THOUGHT I'D DIED AND GONE TO HEAVEN'?** Well we both nearly pinched ourselves to make sure we actually hadn't! The massive empty hall had bright white marble floors, huge sky blue walls that stretched up and up into eternity, and a chandelier the size of an alien spacecraft. For some reason the entire lobby just happened to be devoid of any humans the second we walked in, so the light bouncing off the ceiling, floor and walls was bright enough to make us shade our eyes. You'd have to see it to believe it. It was 'heaven'.

We'll never really know what heaven is like until we're finally there. Everything we try to imagine within our earthly minds is really just pure speculation. Mansions, crowns, wings. One thing we can be sure of, though, is this: we'll get to see Jesus face to face, and worship him forever. If you ask me, that's going to be the best part of all. Until then, I'll just have to be content with asking questions.

God's mind

Now we see God as if we are looking at a reflection in a mirror. But then, in the future, we will see him right before our eyes. Now I know only a part, but at that time I will know fully, as God has known me.
(1 Corinthians 13:12)

I know a man in Christ who was taken up to the third heaven. This happened 14 years ago. I don't know if the man was in his body or out of his body, but God knows. And I know that this

man was taken up to paradise. I don't know if he was in his body or away from his body, but he heard things that he is not able to explain. He heard things that no one is allowed to tell.
(2 Corinthians 12:2–4)

Immediately the Spirit took control of me, and there in heaven was a throne with someone sitting on it. The one sitting there was as beautiful as precious stones, like jasper and carnelian. All around the throne was a rainbow with clear colours like an emerald. In a circle around the throne were 24 other thrones with 24 elders sitting on them. The elders were dressed in white, and they had gold crowns on their heads. Lightning flashes and noises of thunder came from the throne. Before the throne there were seven lamps burning, which are the seven Spirits of God. Also before the throne there was something that looked like a sea of glass, as clear as crystal.
(Revelation 4:2–6)

The wall was made of jasper. The city was made of pure gold, as pure as glass. The foundation stones of the city walls had every kind of expensive jewel in them. The first foundation stone was jasper, the second was sapphire, the third was chalcedony, the fourth was emerald, the fifth was onyx, the sixth was carnelian, the seventh was yellow quartz, the eighth was beryl, the ninth was topaz, the tenth was chrysoprase, the eleventh was jacinth and the twelfth was amethyst. The twelve gates were twelve pearls. Each gate was made from one pearl. The street of the city was made of pure gold, as clear as glass. I did not see a temple in the city. The Lord God All-Powerful and the Lamb were the city's temple. The city did not need the sun or the moon to shine on it. The glory of God gave the city light. The Lamb was the city's lamp. The peoples of the world will walk by the light given by the Lamb. The rulers of the earth will bring their glory into the city. The city's gates will never close on any day, because there is no night there. The greatness and the honour of the nations will be brought into the city. Nothing unclean will ever enter the city. No one who does shameful things or tells lies will ever enter the city. Only those whose names are written in the Lamb's book of life will enter the city.
(Revelation 21:18–27)

Your mind

- **What is the most beautiful sight I've ever seen?**

  ....

  ....

- **How does this compare to what I will see in heaven?**

  ....

  ....

- **Apart from Jesus (too obvious), who's the first person I want to talk to when I get to heaven?**

  ....

  ....

- **How can I start to experience heaven on earth – even right now? (HINT: John 17:3)**

  ....

  ....

Chip Kendall, *The Mind of chipK: Enter at Your Own Risk*, Authentic Media, 2006

CIRCLE:

☺ ☹ 😐 ⊙!⊙ ☺ 😲

TICK:

Total rubbish ☐   Not sure ☐   Worth thinking about ☐   Genius ☐

FILL:

....
....
....
....

Hidden pearls

When you go to heaven you'll be with Jesus.
Right now we just read about Jesus. People in
the Bible got to be with him on earth, but we
look forward to our experience of being with
him in the future,
in heaven.

HEAVEN ON EARTH

Helen talks

Relaxing on a beach in Thailand.

Looking out at a crystal clear ocean.

Craggy sculptural islands jutting out of the water with the promise of exploration and adventure.

The sun warming your skin.

A cool drink.

Your ten favourite people in the world around you . . .

Is that your idea of heaven on earth?

Whatever it is, heaven will be so much better! Lots of people have had visions or dreams of heaven and even near death experiences. There are tales of mansions, green fields, amazing waterfalls and all kinds of other things! Some people's stories of heaven sound a little bit weird and I find myself thinking, 'Hmm, I hope it's not like that!' Is there any way to figure out what it will be like?

We know that God doesn't change, he's the same yesterday, today and forever (Hebrews 13:8), so I reckon we can take a guess at heaven by looking at things we know about God already.

Creativity

God is creative. He made the whole world, with amazing intricate detail and vast sweeping landscapes. Why would he stop? Heaven will be the display case for his most amazing designs!

People

Someone once said to me, the one thing you can take to heaven is people! As we witness and win our friends to Christ, we can be assured that they will be in heaven too. God created us to relate to others and need others, so imagine the biggest get-together/party/celebration and you're probably not even close.

Friendship with Jesus

God loves us and heaven will be our chance to continue the relationship we started with him on earth and take it too the next level. My little boy Cole (who is currently 4 ¾ years old) always asks me, 'When will I be able to give Jesus a big hug?' Heaven is the place!

Imagine
Why not sit back, close your eyes and imagine what heaven will be like. Imagine praising God with total abandon. Imagine the closeness of his presence and the beauty of his creation.

Praise
Let this lead you into praising God for the amazing things he has done in your life.

Read

Check out these verses to inspire you: Revelation 7:15–17, Revelation 22:12–21

ReactionReactionReactionReaction

CIRCLE:

☺ ☹ 😐 😯 😕 😲

TICK:

Total rubbish ☐   Not sure ☐   Worth thinking about ☐   Genius ☐

FILL:

....

....

REALITY CHECK

Mix and match

For this reality check find the best illustration to answer each of these deep questions. Match them up by drawing a line between the two, you can make it as colourful as you like.

a. If God is good then why does he send people to hell?

b. Can everyone go to heaven?

c. Who made God?

d. What does Jesus' death have to do with forgiveness?

e. When does eternal life begin?

f. What counts as sin?

1. How do we tell the time? By looking at a clock. What did people do before clocks were invented? They looked at the sun? Who made the sun? God. The word 'made' involves the concept of time, God exists outside of time, he is eternal so he wasn't made.

2. Every action has a reaction. The laws of the universe teach us this so why should God's other laws be any different? If a law is broken the law breaker must suffer the consequences or there would be no justice. God is a good judge. Christians believe that even though we all deserve to go to hell it doesn't have to be anyone's destination. Instead choose Jesus, choose life.

3. As shocking as it may sound God believes in the death penalty. The pay-cheque for all of our sin is death. In Old Testament times a perfect lamb was sacrificed for the sins of the people. When Jesus died on the cross he paid our death penalty. As the Son of God he's the only human past, present or future who could do this so that we could have forgiveness from God.

4. Jesus said, 'This is eternal life: that people know you, the only true God, and that they can know Jesus Christ, the one you sent' (John 17:3). So if knowing God is eternal life, then eternal life can begin right now. By spending time getting to know God, we've already begun to experience eternal life.

5. Jesus said we cannot see God's kingdom (heaven) unless we are born again (John 3:3). When a couple is expecting a new baby they get a room ready for it to sleep in with everything it needs. God has a room ready in heaven for all those who believe Jesus is the son of God and died for their sins. Accept this invitation and be born again.

6. At some point we've all offended a good friend. That offence creates a barrier between us and them no matter how much we love each other. In the same way when we break God's laws (even in our hearts) that creates a barrier between us and him. Anything that is offensive to God is sin.

(Answers to reality check: a = 2, b = 5, c = 1, d = 3, e = 4, f = 6)

Pray

Lord, thank you for the amazing forgiveness that I can find through Jesus' death on the cross. Thank you that despite all the things I do that don't match up to your perfect standard, I can still be with you now and in heaven because of Jesus' sacrifice. Please help me to show my non-Christian friends and family what a loving, forgiving and just God you are. Help me always to be ready with an answer about you and help me show grace and forgiveness to others as you have shown it to me.

In Jesus' name,

Amen.